A Shared Journey

FOR
GEORGE AND KRISTI

A Shared Journey
The Birth of a Child

Donni Betts

CELESTIAL ARTS
Millbrae, California

Illustrations by Pedro J. Gonzalez
Cover Photo by George Betts
Interior Photos by Jo Dahlin, George Betts, Viddie Vargas,
George Dunkin, Don Lawless and Donni Betts

Copyright © 1977 by Celestial Arts

Published by Celestial Arts
231 Adrian Road
Millbrae, California 94030

First printing, March 1977
Made in the United States of America

Library of Congress Cataloging in Publication Data

Betts, Donni.
    A shared journey.

    1. Pregnancy—Psychological aspects.   2. Child-
birth—Psychological aspects.   3. Parent and child.
4. Mothers—Biography.   5. Betts, Donni.   I. Title.
RG560.B47   612.6′3   76-53347
ISBN 0-89087-146-9

1 2 3 4 5 6 7 — 82 81 80 79 78 77

Preface

Someday you may ask me how you came to be, and I want you to know that you were created in a moment of love, at a perfect time. Your father and I knew we were ready to share ourselves with a child, and from the very moment you were created, we knew you were going to be. We were so sure, in fact, that we got all dressed up and went out to our favorite restaurant to celebrate.

The next day, your father was telling some friends, "Donni is pregnant." They asked when you would be born, and he confidently told them, "In nine months." And he was right. You were born exactly nine months from the day you were conceived.

So, with excitement we counted the days until I could have a test to verify what we already knew: that we were going to have a baby. When the day came we were in San Francisco on vacation, and went to a clinic to have the test. I waited for the results, fidgeting anxiously. When the nurse said, "The test was positive, Mrs. Betts. You're pregnant," I began to cry uncontrollable tears of joy. We spent a wondeful day, sharing a special closeness as the realization of what your presence would mean to us was now more than just a dream.

Oh yes, we knew in our hearts that you were going to be, and yet hearing the words made it a joyful reality for both of us. And so the journey your father and I have shared became a journey to be shared by three. This is the story of your beginning, your journey to become a person, our first meeting, how we grew to become a family. This is the story of you. . .

By sharing your story with others, I hope that some may gain reassurance and insight into their own shared journey of pregnancy and birth, and others who have never experienced this miracle firsthand may acquire some understanding of what the whole process is all about. . .

July 3

A beginning—

At last I've slowed down, relaxed enough to put a few of my feelings down. So much has happened; so many feelings, experiences and changes. I'm overwhelmed, overstimulated, still unable to sort out the many things that have happened.

I feel cheated: when we left two weeks ago, summer hadn't yet arrived. We came home yesterday to a blazing, oppressive heat, and I never got to see the summer begin.

I feel like a storybook case of pregnancy: today I felt fat, ugly and dirty, but lacking energy to do anything about it. My breasts seem to be growing larger day by day; lovely, but they're too sore to be touched.

I feel concern for George: he's getting so excited about "Rocky Jr." which thrills me, but how much fun can I be, between my extreme moods, queer tastes, sore breasts, queasy stomach, lack of energy or enthusiasm, and weight gain. And yet he's so patient (most of the time), involved, concerned, and even a little protective. I couldn't ask for more.

We went for a bike ride tonight, and saw a fireworks display. My mind went reeling back in time to what seems like countless Fourth-of-July's at Grandma's house in the country. It was always a time for a family reunion, with snakes and sparklers, and my cousins taunting me for being afraid of the firecrackers. And when night finally came, we'd all go out by the side lawn, and Dad and my uncle would start the fireworks display in the dirt road. And I would always bring my Teddy Bear out to watch and whisper to him that it was all in his honor, because it was his birthday. I got him 22 years ago tomorrow. . .

They say that in pregnancy you do a lot of reminiscing about your own childhood. It already seems true for me. They also say you become more aware of smells, which I noticed on our ride.

And now I'm anxious to see a doctor, to help bring this into focus. It doesn't seem quite real yet. And I'm anxious to clean the house and get lots of exercise and eat well and lose some of the weight I've gained and bake some bread; just kind of settle in and feel at home and away from the world all together. I don't want to see or be with anyone but George. And I want some time alone too. I feel like pampering myself, and doing all kinds of feminine things.

July 4

He's a nightcrawler,
        this one I live with—
avoiding as much of the day
as he can, through sleep,
greeting the darkness
        with abundant energy
            and excessive restlessness. . .

I'm angry tonight.

Frustrated, angry and lonely.

At nothing in particular and everything in general.

I have a headache, I have gas, the house stinks, I feel fat and I should lose weight, I'm hungry, I don't like the way you take care of things. In a week you still haven't put the suitcases away.

My boobs are sagging. . .already.

Some thoughts:

You are never just "a little" pregnant. Once you conceive, your body immediately begins a major upheaval, and your mind too. But the changes come instantly—all of a sudden it's *there*!

It's hard to believe there's a *person* growing in me. It could just as easily be a cat or a grapefruit, or nothing at all. But a person?

There is already a great difference between the *fantasy* of being pregnant, and the *reality*. Always I have thought there was nothing more romantic and beautiful than a pregnant woman. HA! So far it's been some sickness, depression, fear and insecurity, mixed with joy and excitement (which has been somewhat tremulous—don't count your chickens before they're hatched).

I walked into a maternity shop today for the first time. I wanted to turn and run. It might as well have been a shop for men's underwear—it seemed so strange. I know it's awfully early to buy any clothes, but I needed to look. Somehow just being there made it more of a reality for me. I feel a need for some reality, something I can grasp. I haven't seen a doctor yet. I think that would help a lot.

July 8

Today, for no reason at all, I had to cry. And cry and cry. Hormones, I guess. But I asked you just to laugh at me and let me go ahead. I knew if you took it all seriously or thought something was really wrong, then I would too. So you laughed at me, and held me, and you were patient and seemed to understand, until finally I was finished, and we laughed at me, together.

July 11

Twins? . . . I saw a doctor today because I've been having some mild cramping. He said it could be the unaccustomed feelings of being pregnant, or a threatening miscarriage. He didn't seem overly concerned, so I'm trying not to be either. But it's hard not to think about it.

I got the first anticipated rush of pleasure I've been waiting for when he said, "Well, you're definitely pregnant!" He also told me there is no way I'm only seven or eight weeks along; more like ten or twelve weeks. . .unless it's twins. I *know* there's no way I could have been pregnant that long. I don't know how, but I just know.

So many things are happening. . .
So many changes
    both physical and emotional,
everything moving so swiftly
that I feel my pen
    can't keep up with it all.

I can't quite believe what is happening to me. According to *my* calculations, I'm seven weeks pregnant today. But already I can't zip up *any* of my pants. I don't seem to be getting fat anywhere else, but lying in the bathtub today, I noticed a small, barely perceptible bulge very low in my abdomen. A friend came by today and showed me how to feel my enlarging uterus. It was a wild sensation, like a kind of growth, which is just what it is, in a way. She is going to make a blouse for me. I hope she hurries, because I think I'm going to need it pretty soon. All that reassurance I so longed for a few days ago is quickly coming to reality.

July 15

I feel good again! For so long I felt tired and queasy and just
unable to cope with the ordinary functions of living. But all of
a sudden my energy level is rising, and so are my spirits! I
started Transcendental Meditation three days ago, so it's too
soon to say it has brought about the changes. But I believe the
extra rest it provides could be a part of it. How nice it will be
for the baby and me to sit down and completely relax for 20
minutes two or three times a day. I think it will really help.

I feel the days passing steadily, each one so essential in the
development of this unborn child. And knowing this makes it
easier to slow down and be less anxious.

July 16

Tomorrow I go for my first official check-up. I'm really
anxious to get it over, and have some questions answered,
like when it's due, etc.

The hardest thing for me to accept is the way I feel I affect
other people, especially George and others who are close to
me. I've never spent so much time thinking about myself. It
makes me uncomfortable. At times I seem to be turning
inward. I notice it especially when I'm around others. All of a
sudden I'll realize someone has been talking and I haven't
heard a word they've said.

I feel lazy sometimes, like there are so many things I'd like
to be doing but I just seem to have energy to do the daily
things. But I feel like I *could* do more—like I'm spinning my
wheels. Sometimes I think I'm taking advantage of my
"condition." I hope not. I try to be aware enough so that I
won't.

I wonder . . .
How am I to cope
with my changing body,
my changing life?
Most of the time
I am able to accept
the changes,
flow with them
and be happy about them.

But sometimes I feel
out of control . . .
All these changes
are going to occur
of their own accord.
It seems there is nothing
I can do, either to help
or hinder
the process.

How do I accept
so much change?
I can no longer
be a little girl . . .
I'll be the mother . . .
so much of my time
and energy
will no longer be spent
as I choose,
but as someone else demands.

I've never had to face
      many demands before.

I know
      I chose this road.
         I don't want to change it
and yet sometimes
      when I think of tomorrow
         I feel overwhelmed . . .

There is something joyful
    and mysterious
in the re-creation of life.

Everyone I meet,
    friends, strangers,
        mothers, young boys,
        teenage girls,

everyone,
    seems caught up in
      a kind of celebration
and wanting to be a part,
    wanting to share
      in our joy
        and anticipation.

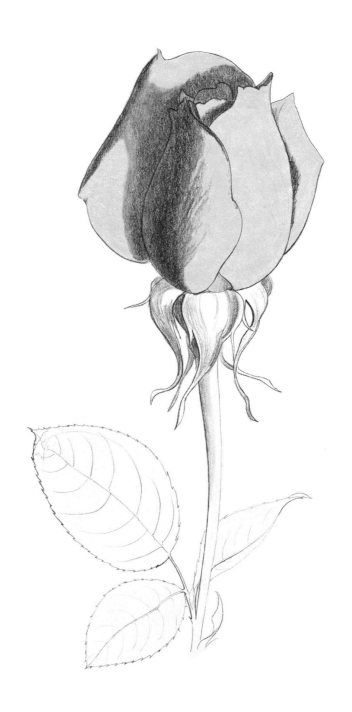

October 7

I haven't written for two months and as I look back over what I've written before, it's hard to believe all the changes, both inside and outside. I'm four and a half months along, and although things are still sometimes frightening, I'm mostly aware of feelings of anticipation, excitement & wonder.

Dr. Bradley is a dynamo. After reading his book, *Husband Coached Childbirth* I knew I would never be happy with any other doctor. After meeting him for the first time I knew I had made the right choice for me. His method allows us to experience the birth together, unmedicated, prepared and educated, through lectures and exercise classes.

George seems enthusiastic but not yet too involved in the idea of being a part of the birth. He has so much on his mind, and I'm sure it seems like a long way off.

He's so excited about the baby though. He speaks of it constantly, enthusiastically. He's so gentle, considerate with me . . . more so than usual. He's learned to control his quick tongue and sudden temper. He's so aware, and when I sometimes feel trapped and panicky, like my life is closing in around me, he's quick to reassure me we can work together to see that our life together remains exciting. Sometimes I have the uncanny feeling that he senses my mood, my feelings, even before I do, and knows exactly what to do, how to react. I'm so lucky . . .

Three weeks ago during my meditation I first became aware of the small life stirring within me. Low in my abdomen I felt two thumps. It was so exciting I came right out of the meditation. I've felt movement every day since then. At first it was indistinguishable from intestinal rumblings and muscle twitches. Then a week ago, again during meditation, I felt three kicks so hard that I gasped, started. The next night in bed, George had his hand on my stomach, and HE gasped! Since then I've had no trouble feeling the movement. I usually feel it when I'm sitting, and often when I'm lying or standing motionless. I haven't felt it as much yesterday or today, and I miss it. It's like a form of communication.

Yesterday I spent the whole day with lots of people, and when I finally crawled in bed I became aware of something I've been doing unconsciously since I first felt the baby move. Several times a day (not during TM) I take a few minutes to tune out the world and just feel in touch with the baby. I become aware of the weight in my abdomen, its movements, and lately I've even startled to put my hand on my stomach, directly on my skin if possible, the better to feel the move-ment. And all unconsciously. But last night in bed I realized I hadn't taken time for this. It was kind of an empty feel-ing . . . I missed it.

October 10

I sometimes feel this is one of the most peaceful, contented periods of my life. In that way I wish it would never end.

At times it seems I've carried a baby in me a thousand times. I think it has something to do with the subconscious, ancient, animal part of our brain. Something that draws me back to the beginning of life, a common experience, buried so deeply that it's almost below the level of conscious aware-ness. I think it may be this bond, this unconscious knowledge which gives pregnant women a look of peace and content-ment.

I wish more people were anxious to feel the baby move. Maybe they're just shy and don't know how to ask, or think that I wouldn't like it. It's such an exciting feeling, I'm eager to share it.

October 11

I've read so often of the many emotional changes a woman experiences during pregnancy, some of which I blatantly assured myself were old wives' tales, not for me to worry about. I was sure that if a woman were truly happy about pregnancy, she could escape those silly doubts about her desirability and sexual attractiveness. She would never have to worry about her changing body, or cope with the possibility of feeling just plain unappealing.

Well, now I realize how naive those assumptions really are. I thought they were based on looks, on externals, when in reality it's much more basic than that. I know now that I do experience such feelings from time to time, no matter how happy I feel about being pregnant. These feelings come from a much deeper source: my feelings about my own self-image.

I think that at this point in my life more than any other, my concept of the way I see myself is more threatened than it's ever been before. I look forward to being a mother, and at the same time, as I become more aware of the demands, I realize I don't want to be "just" a mother. I want to be recognized as a person with potential and talents for so many more things, such as my ability to work with and relate to people. And because I feel a potential threat to this recognition like I've never known before, I'm forced to face it and deal with it. And I can feel something going on within me. I am coming to terms with myself, I am fighting for my individuality, I am taking steps to assert myself. I am talking and writing more freely and spontaneously about my feelings; I am drawing more on my creative potential; I am becoming more assertive.

In other words, being pregnant has provided me with a

stimulus I don't believe I would have found otherwise, and because of it I am becoming stronger, more of a person in my own right; and by my own means—accomplishing exactly what I want—the opposite of what I feared. I have begun to use my fear as a creative tool . . .

October 20

Tonight I feel detached from my body, as if it wasn't my own. My stomach is distended, and people are making cracks about my rear (which used to be, well, if not *tiny,* at least *small*) being the same way. How depressing . . . will I *ever* feel like the same person again?

I've been having nightmares and otherwise strange dreams. Hormones I'm sure, but it makes me dread going to sleep . . .

I get a little overwhelmed when I realize things will NEVER be the same again . . . and yet it seems like this child isn't really something new in our lives, but someone who has always been with us, silently . . .

We are so close now, our relationship carrying a new, special meaning—a new dimension has been added and we have something even better than we've had before. It shows in so many little ways: an extra touch or word of encouragement, a little extra attention paid to each other, our patience expanded. We share more passing, inner feelings—again, little things that have more meaning, new importance.

October 27

You've been away four days now, and I hardly miss you at all—as long as I don't think about you too much. But if I think of you, it's a painful feeling . . . our house is so silent, lacking the energy and vitality you give. It's a mixed feeling for me—peaceful, and yet a little empty. And yet it makes me more aware than ever of how much I love you, and love sharing my life with you. . .

I feel vulnerable without you.
You give me so much protection,
just by your presence. . .

I have never met anyone
        in my life who
        compares to you.
You give me so much
        just by being yourself,
        and I love every part
            of you.
Missing you,
        feeling the loss of you
        not being here,
makes me cherish you
        all the more.
Please. . . hurry home. . .

I feel a new kind of
security while you're away,
for each time I feel
your baby move inside me,
I realize a part of you
is always with me.

I feel so . . . pregnant! Like all those weird mood changes have suddenly hit me at once. I'm depressed over nothing. I feel like withdrawing from everyone except George, our friend Viddie and our parents. I feel like a puppy starved for affection and attention.

I get upset about things far beyond anything rational. It upsets me to no end if George leaves one little thing out of place, or wears jeans when I want him to get dressed up.

I almost feel like a caricature of myself. I have no control over my emotions. I cry with no provocation at *all*. And all because of some silly hormones. I feel like I'm going crazy.

Some of the funny little things I'm starting to notice: my stomach is like a balloon with a message written on it that you can't read until it's all blown up. As the skin stretches, I'm discovering all kinds of little scars and marks I've never seen before.

I'm beginning to understand what people mean about being awkward when you're pregnant. Try to get out of a little car, or even out of bed, with a bowling ball in your lap; not too easy, let alone graceful. By the same token, try lying on your back with that same bowling ball in place. Or just try to get in a comfortable position in bed.

I also find I have to eat less and less. . . more and more often! There just isn't as much room to put food as there used to be, but my body is demanding more of it. And sometimes I get what's called the "heartburn of pregnancy," which for me is a gasey, burning sensation from my throat down to my stomach, like I have to burp, but can't. I've never had it before, and it seems to be aggravated by one bite of _anything_, or by lying down flat.

I find I am able to summon less energy each day. I guess that's because I'm approaching the last trimester, when my body is really working hard and carrying a heavy load. (Wow, the time is going fast!) My legs get tired and sometimes ache. But I've been aware of the fact that this would happen and I've tried to prepare for it: I'm trying to get all my Christmas running around out of the way now, collecting materials for some do-it-yourself things at home, like jewelry and macramé. I'm learning to work some rest time into my schedule, and just not do as much as I'm used to.

I still have weird dreams once in a while. I still cry sometimes for what seems like no reason. But I'm beginning to realize there _is_ a reason, although it's not always easy to be sure what it is. Dr. Bradley says there is extra fluid in the body which puts pressure on the brain, and that can cause some bizarre reactions.

Another thing that tells me the baby is growing is that I

can feel it progressing upward in my belly. I can tell because when I first felt it kick it was really low, near my pelvic bone, and now I'm feeling movement near my belly button.

Some women have had some things they just couldn't stand to eat or even smell, like meat. Unfortunately, I still love almost everything! The only thing I still dislike is alcohol. Up until about a week ago I couldn't wear perfume. I liked to smell it on other people, but I couldn't stand to wear it. Now all of a sudden I want to wear it all the time. I also have suddenly become more concerned about my appearance. I want to look nice all the time, especially around George. It's like I want to go back to the time when our life was most romantic and intimate; only natural to want to hold onto that, when I think of the incredible change about to take place. So for now, I want to be wined and dined and romanced, and made to feel I'm every bit as desirable with a pot belly and round face. All those silly things I've read about in the books and *knew* that *I'd* never feel!

It's so much fun now with people poking my stomach, trying to guess if it's a boy or girl and when it will come, offering suggestions for names (usually their own!). Everyone likes to get into the act.

The thought of a potential crisis causes a myriad of reactions.

There is a possibility that our blood types, being incompatible, could cause more problems for the baby at birth, such as jaundice or anemia. Which simply means to me that the baby may not have the best possible start in the world.

My initial reaction was fear, but I quickly checked my imagination from running wild. My practical side coming out I guess; we still have three months to go, and if I spent the whole time worrying I would be a nervous wreck by then. I can only do my best to eat well and follow Dr. Bradley's exercises. He says they promote better circulation and lessen the chance of mixing the mother and the baby's blood.

I am so thankful we changed to Dr. Bradley. I have complete confidence in his ability to do all he possibly can; or all _anyone_ can. He is the best. We can't ask for more.

Being concerned about the baby has brought us even closer. Somehow the bond is strengthened even more. And I told George that realizing the baby is vulnerable has all of a sudden made it seem more of a reality. Suddenly I can believe there really is a _person_ inside me who will emerge and have to survive and deal with the world by its own means, rather than being dependent on the life-giving support of my body. A funny kind of reality check, but strangely, I like the feeling.

A funny thing happened. There is a test you can do with a needle on a piece of thread. Someone slides the thread up and down on the outside of your upturned hand a few times and then holds it over your palm, being careful not to touch your hand with the needle. If the needle moves back and forth, it's a boy; in a circular motion, it's a girl. Not only that, if you continue and repeat the whole thing until the needle will no longer move when suspended over your palm, it will tell you how many children you will have, and the sex of each, in order, from first to last. We tried it a week ago and the needle said boy, boy, girl. Then someone else tried it on me tonight and it was boy (changing to girl in the middle), boy, girl. Interesting. Then we tried it on several friends who have had children, and each time it came out right. We even tried it on our dog, Katy, and it was right—all eight times!

November 25

Someone asked me today if I'm anxious for the baby to be here. But I'm not ready. I think nature planned the nine months as a preparation not only for the baby, but for me, to have time to make the psychological adjustment from being a "little girl" to being a mother.

I've experienced a whole range of emotions since I've first known you were going to be, baby: uncertainty, apprehension, excitement, joy. But until last night I hadn't felt the sense of intense, overpowering love that came to me as I felt your nightly stirrings. Suddenly, for the first time, I felt you as real, a complete person contained in a two-pound little body; all the potential for your whole life already there, inside me. And knowing that, and that you are a part of me, I love you in a way I've never loved before.

My energy is slowly being consumed.
Fatigue comes more quickly.
A simple task
        becomes a monumental effort.
My body is slowing down
while my mind races ahead,
anxious to finish the
        Christmas shopping
or work on any number
of little projects
        which are beginning
to seem like big projects.

The most difficult part
        to accept
is that my mind and body
        seem to be running
            at different speeds.
And yet I feel a serenity,
        a calmness,
a deep happiness which seems to show on my
        face,
for many people have
        told me so.
They say I'm prettier . . .

Someone asked me a while ago if I'm afraid of the actual birth experience and my answer was, without hesitation, "No." It hadn't even occurred to me to be afraid. I have complete confidence in Dr. Bradley, the Bradley method, in George as my coach, and in myself.

Since then I've thought about it a lot. The time is drawing nearer, and I still feel no fear. I'm curious, wondering if "our" labor will go quickly, take forever, or go quickly but *seem* like forever. I am anxious to know how much it will hurt, how much I can control the pain and if I'll really be able to have a natural, drugless childbirth. Most of all, I wonder if it will really be, for us, the peak experience I have heard it described to be.

We were talking the other night—what if we should be one of the unlucky couples whose baby isn't normal? I think the hardest thing for both of us to handle would be a child who is mentally retarded. Any other type of defect would be tragic, but retardation, for me, would be the most tragic of all. Then George said something incredible, yet true. When we thought of these things our concern wasn't for the child who would bear such an affliction, but for ourselves: how would *we* handle it?

I have always wondered what it would *feel* like to be pregnant: if all my organs would feel pushed around, if I could actually *feel* the baby. Well, I feel pretty much the same, except that my stomach feels like it's pushed up and awfully crowded, which it is. Although I'm sometimes aware of a heavy dragging sensation very low, around the abdomen, I don't actually feel the baby's presence unless it moves. Otherwise it just feels like more of *me*.

It's really an effort to bend over—imagine you just ate Thanksgiving dinner, your clothes are too tight, you're sitting

in the car with a bowling ball in your lap and you just
dropped your glove. Now try to bend over. That pretty much
describes the feeling . . .

I feel so overwhelmed. I've been reading some books that
describe the atmosphere in the home of a newborn infant.
The books are good in that they help make me aware of the
possible conflict and pressures that can arise, but they deal
with only the negative aspects. And they go into it in such
detail that it has disturbed me all day to the point of
wondering "How will I live through it?" and "Why did I
want a child so much if it's going to interfere so drastically
with my own life and my relationship with George?"

Just writing about it (George's suggestion this time) helps
me to get it in perspective again. All day I've felt kind of low,
overwhelmed at times, trapped. I've tried to fight my way out
of it by seeing it as a challenge, thinking of new ways to
handle situations I haven't been faced with yet, realizing how
much support I have and how lucky I am. I even made a
mental list of all my assets. And yet somehow I couldn't
shake this awful feeling—I couldn't seem to overcome it,
until finally George noticed how quiet I've been and asked if I
was down. And boom, there was a flood of tears, out it came
and it was like a cleansing to be rid of the feeling of carrying a
burden single-handed.

The happiest time of the year, and yet I feel at an all-time
low. I worked so long, at such a feverish pace to have
everything ready for Christmas, and I finished nearly a week
early. I planned, literally for months, so that I would have the
time and energy to make special gifts, and buy those I didn't
make. I'm glad I thought ahead, because now I don't have the
energy to become a part of the traditional Christmas Rush.

And yet it's such a letdown. It's like I'm experiencing the after-Christmas "blahs" ahead of time. And even when I think of something to do, I don't want to do it. I feel listless, disinterested.

I'm anxious to get going on the baby's room, get things ready and in order. I feel resistance: George isn't ready, his mother doesn't want us to buy things—well, practically until the baby comes. It's my nature to be prepared in advance. Then I can relax. But I wonder if it won't be worse to be ready and waiting for the baby than for Christmas . . .

There are times when I'm anxious for the baby to be here. I want to _know_ this person who will be such a part of our lives . . . for the rest of our lives. And yet there are times when I feel I'll be pregnant forever—times I want to capture the feeling, to feel the closeness we share now as a single unit, the protective feeling I get from knowing that I alone am creating the total world for this tiny being, inside. At these times, I'm aware of how good my experience has been: so free of the complaints of many women in their last trimester such as varicose veins, backache, hemorrhoids, difficulty in breathing or sleeping. I do tire easily, something I'm not accustomed to. I no longer feel as though I must accomplish as much as I normally would. I'm re-evaluating my needs and priorities, and I'm finally beginning to slow down, gracefully. I do experience frustration at times, when I have difficulty tying my shoes, or I'm too tired by 10:00 a.m. to curl my hair. I may still cry or get angry, but the way I feel inside about the frustration is somehow different.

Something funny (well, not *funny* really—odd is a better
way of putting it) seems to be taking place. I am re-experienc-
ing the nausea of the first three months, especially when my
stomach is empty. Today I lost my breakfast and lunch. I
think it's because the baby is getting bigger and taking more
and more nourishment to supply its own needs.

Time seems to be running short—this time has really
passed so quickly for me. Only six weeks until our due date
(but Dr. Bradley says eighty percent of all babies are born two
weeks late, so I'm trying to set my sights past that magical
day on the calendar so I won't be disappointed or fidgety).
There seems to be so much to do, both in getting ready for the
baby's arrival and homecoming, and just to be more organized around the house.

George has been a big help, cleaning out his den for the
baby to use, and helping me make preparations. And he's
really getting excited about being a coach. I know he'll be
wonderful at it: his voice is so soothing in helping me relax,
and with his encouragement I can already hold my breath as
long as I'm supposed to be able to. We both want so much to
be ready and prepared.

And yet I wonder if I'll get everything done that I want to
accomplish. Viddie is planning to come in and help after the
baby comes. I am so glad to have her help, and yet because
she's a friend and doesn't know what's involved when a
newborn is around, I'm afraid of her feeling used, or like
she's a maid . . .

Yesterday's visit to Dr. Bradley was an event. He was in
rare form, talking, and taking time to explain some details we
didn't know, having missed the last lecture. George asked if
he could hear the heartbeat and Dr. Bradley was so patient in
finding it with his fetoscope, making sure we heard it. What

an incredible sound, that rapid thump thump!

Then he compared it with my own beat, slow in comparison, explaining that a hummingbird's heart beats much faster than an elephant's. And I agreed—I *am* beginning to feel like an elephant!

Another pleasant experience last night was meeting a couple with two young children. They admitted they not only enjoy their children, but learn from them as well. How refreshing after the articles I've been reading which relate the drastic, undesirable changes a child renders in the lives and relationship of a couple. Without fail these articles have painted such a negative, almost hopeless view of parenthood that I would walk around for a whole day feeling that my own life was about to end, as well as my relationship with George.

But to our relief, this couple were proof that things don't have to be as dim as the articles suggest.

January 9

I wonder if you will ever know the joy and anticipation that we've been sharing in preparing for your arrival. We've felt so much excitement in painting, cleaning, shopping and getting your room ready for you. It makes you seem like more of a reality, a real person.

In some ways your birth still seems so long away. It's hard to believe that each day brings you closer to being *with* us, instead of only a part of me.

I find myself praying more and more, "Please, let this be a healthy baby." The more I think of you, the more I fear for your health; and how we would handle a crisis.

You have the hiccups, and I'm smiling inwardly, delighted at the thought that we are sharing a secret no one else can know. I feel so close to you . . . this is a such a special time . . . you are almost an independent person, ready to be a part of the world of other people. Yet at this point it's just the two of us, still one, sharing something so delicate, barely tangible. Maybe that's why it's so special.

As this special time is coming close to the end, I am becoming more aware of every movement you make. I cherish each fluttering, realizing that soon I'll be without the gentle reminder that someone else is always with me.

The other night we went to the hospital for the tour the father must take before he can be allowed in the delivery room. It was an exciting trip, once again bringing you closer to reality. We saw the labor rooms, what fathers wear, and most exciting to us, we saw the newborn babies.

I can only marvel at how perfect those babies are; that when they are born they are complete! What is even more wondrous to me is that if you were born right now, you too would be perfect and complete. I think that somehow I had the notion that babies arrive not quite finished, looking not quite human.

I am so glad we are preparing for this incredible event. Together we have practiced relaxation and deep abdominal breathing for first stage labor and, prolonged breath-holding delivery. Plus all sorts of other exercises to strengthen my back and Kegel muscle, improve my posture, and just generally to make life a little easier.

I am moving slower and with increased effort now. I sometimes even lose my balance for the simple reason that

I'm front-heavy and carrying around forty extra pounds. When I get discouraged at moving so slow I try to imagine how I would feel if I constantly had to carry a forty-pound pack, and I realize how well I'm really doing. Now the smallest little jaunt to a shopping center becomes the major expedition of the day, something I must literally plan my day around.

All my clothes are getting too tight, and I'm becoming limited in what I can wear. Blouses are too tight in the arms and stomach and I've had to clip the elastic in my pant waistbands (the ones I haven't worn the seat out of!). I'm not really tired of the clothes, but a little tired of being big. In the beginning I would never have believed the time would come when I would longingly think of my "skinny" clothes, but they are suddenly becoming very important. They represent the goal I am already psyching myself for: to get back to my normal 110 pounds as soon as possible, which right now is seemingly impossible. But I'm determined . . .

I hate to be around you when I'm like this. I feel so ugly and smelly and fat, and I just can't seem to stop crying. I don't know why.

The tears keep coming and release feels good, but at the same time I feel guilty that you have to put up with all this. Even though you're patient and understanding, I know how tiresome I must be. Sometimes I just want to be left alone to cry it out. Afterwards I feel like I will be more calm and peaceful.

The other night in our childbirth class the teacher was pointing out a similarity between labor contractions and waves in the ocean. When you look at the waves from shore, they seem huge, too big to be handled. But when you venture in and become at ease, you learn how the waves come in, how to ride with them and flow. And so it is with each contraction. But once in a while you can get caught off guard by a wave. Maybe you aren't paying attention when the wave hits. It knocks you over, and for a moment you feel as though you'll never regain your balance. You come up spluttering, coughing, nose and eyes burning, overwhelmed.

But the important thing is that soon you forget, you're concentrating on riding each wave, flowing again. It's the same in labor. Each contraction is like a wave, and though you may not ride each one perfectly, you are able to regain your balance and be in control, ready for the next one.

It's a beautiful concept, and you (George) loved it so much that you have equated it to life, each day being a wave. Today, I feel as though I wasn't ready for the wave. It swept over me, and no matter how I try I can't seem to regain my balance.

January 23

Up until last night I couldn't quite conceive of the importance of having someone to coach me during labor. But now the baby has dropped, and I am often awakened during the night by the force of my uterus contracting, warming up, getting ready for the "big game." I didn't want to wake you and I tried to relax, but it was almost impossible to do alone. I got up, walked around, did some pelvic rocks, tailor sat and was ready to take a hot bath, when finally the cramping sensation subsided enough to allow me to lie down and go back to sleep. I'm more thankful than ever that you'll be with me. I realize how much I need you . . . and want you.

January 24

A curious thing is happening. We have removed the books and clutter from the den, painted and scrubbed it. Now it's become the nursery, accumulating the paraphernalia necessary for a new baby. The change is more than physical though. Already the room is assuming a personality. I was upset today and went in there to write. As soon as I stepped into the room a calmness enveloped me, soothing me.

January 26

I still haven't really learned to slow down, and today I'm having to pay for it!
Yesterday we spent the whole day at our old college town, visiting friends, revisiting old haunts, and walking, walking,

walking. I knew at the time it was too much, but I continued to push, not wanting to miss anything. Today I awoke feeling stiff and sore from pulled muscles, tired, depressed, overwhelmed. I knew I would pay physically but the emotional frustration is worse.

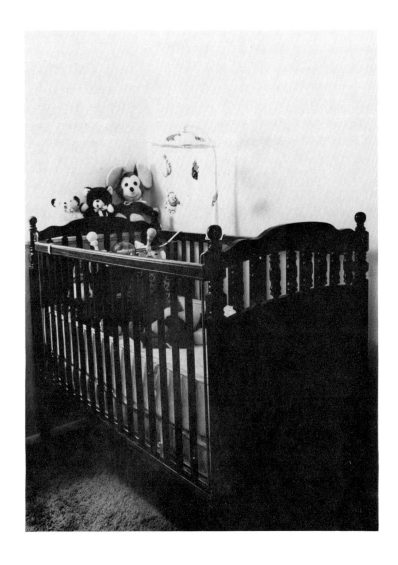

This time is coming to a close so quickly. Last June, it seemed as though an eternity would have to pass before February would arrive. And now, looking back, June could have been yesterday.

Although I'm full of anticipation, excited to meet the baby and get acquainted, I'm not really in a hurry for this special period of my life to end. It's a time of rapid change and adjustment, in the social sense even more than the physical sense. And the changes are so drastic and occur in such a relatively short time span that I'm fully aware of many of them. In our daily living I think change is normally such a slow, gradual process that we are hardly aware of it when it takes place.

I love being involved in observing these shifts in attitude. It's exciting to realize I'm not stagnating, but rearranging. Frightening as it may be at times, it's also exhilarating.

It's taken so long to accept that there really will be another person sharing our world. In the beginning we were often warned that having a baby would change our lifestyle. Immediately our defenses would go up and we would reassure the person that it wouldn't change us at all, that the child would just have to adapt to us. I still believe that, to an extent. We won't deny our individuality. But now I realize that we can't deny our child's individuality, either. We will all make adjustments in learning to live together.

I was so determined not to let anyone cramp my style, that as I thought of things I love to do, I would wonder if the baby would limit me. If I felt it would be impossible to do something, I would make mental plans to leave the baby with someone else. No way would I give up my freedom!

But my feelings are beginning to change. Almost as if by instinct I'm gaining insight into so many concepts I never before would have considered.

Dr. Bradley is a big supporter of breastfeeding, to say the least. I went along with the idea, somewhat unenthusiastically, simply because it was expected of me. The idea sounded fine in theory, but the thought of actually doing it was a little repulsive. I talked to some women, most of whom had tried to nurse, became discouraged and gave up. I learned that none of their doctors had supported them in their effort to nurse. I have been reading all I could get my hands on, as I became more curious about the idea. I enjoyed one book especially: *Nursing Your Baby* by Karen Pryor. From her I began to feel that nursing not only is natural, but can be a most peaceful and nurturing experience for everyone. She stresses the importance of having a pediatrician who is knowledgable about and supportive of breastfeeding. Many doctors know so little about the subject that they encourage mothers to quit at the first sign of difficulty, often needlessly. La Leche League have also been most helpful to me.

By now I am so convinced it is what I want to do that I don't plan to buy any baby bottles. There was one single experience which convinced me more than all the books and talking could ever do, and that was watching one friend successfully nursing her two-week old daughter. I felt such a peacefulness and overwhelming love between those two, and I knew I would be cheating George and our baby as well as myself, if I missed that experience.

Last night at Dr. Bradley's final lecture I saw a girl I'd met a few months before. She was beginning to blossom, and as we compared notes I asked when she was due. She said May first, and my first reaction was to say "Oh, then you still have quite a while to go." But I recalled how often I had heard those words, particularly at her stage, and remembered how belittled I had felt. I'm not sure why. But the memory was enough to make me swallow my words. Instead, I asked her if the time was passing quickly for her, and when she answered "More quickly than I'd like," I distinctly remembered feeling that way at six months too.

I've been so lucky, suffering so few discomforts, even in this last month. There have been times when I thought I couldn't endure pregnancy another day, because the baby's position would put pressure on my stomach, making it impossible to put anything on it, or on my diaphragm, making every breath difficult and painful. But eventually the baby moves and the discomfort goes away and I feel fine again.

Several years ago I began to suffer pain in my lower back. I went to an orthopedic surgeon who informed me that I have several abnormalities in my back. He prescribed exercises to relieve the pain and help correct some of the problem. The exercises helped somewhat, but the pain has always persisted. The doctor also informed me that if I ever became pregnant I would need the support of a maternity corset to help me through the last difficult months. Ha! Not only have I *not* felt the need for such a contraption, but my back feels better now than in the three years before I became pregnant! I am convinced that my pelvic rocking and staying off my feet more are the main reasons, thanks to Dr. Bradley!

Even now I sometimes find it difficult to believe this bulge in my stomach is going to result in a person . . . and very soon! I've forgotten how it feels to have a flat stomach. It seems natural that I should go on like this indefinitely, or that someday the bulge will just sort of fade away.

The time couldn't possibly be so close! Somehow I should feel like we're building up to a big finale, but I don't . . .

Tonight is a turning point
    in our lives
We have spent the last
    five years
    loving each other,
       no cares
         or responsibilities,
           an extended childhood.
But the last two months
have been extra special.
We have given our love
    and attention to each other
almost exclusively.
No work,
    no demands upon us
    from the world.
Tomorrow the vacation ends.
You will return to your world
    of work, schedules,
       expectations.
And soon I too will be
    involved in the demands
      and schedules
    of motherhood.
From this night on
we will not know a time
of total,
    unconcerned solitude.
I'm not really sad
about it at all,
just a little awed

at the thought
that when we wake
tomorrow
our lives will take a step
forward,
there will be no
turning back
to a time such as this . . .

I can almost remember the exact moment when my answer to the often-asked question "Are you ready for the baby to be here?" changed from "Oh no, I'm not in a hurry to rush this experience," to "Yes!"

It seems as though everything came to a peak all at once: everything in readiness, the baby's room just the way we want it, George's long vacation coming to an abrupt end, feeling confident with our role in the birth process. And suddenly I am tired of carrying all this extra weight, being slow, tired. I am ready to meet this person I have been so close to since it's beginning.

I haven't felt awfully uncomfortable, and any discomfort I have felt has been endurable because I know the reward is so close.

Yet both of us have the strange feeling that all of this will never culminate; the room won't really be occupied by a real person, a part of our family; I'll still be pregnant, months from now. It's so hard to grasp the reality, to believe that we could be parents by tomorrow . . .

I've been having more and more activity in my uterus (not pains, but contractions, as I've learned to call them). It feels just like menstrual cramps, lasting from one to two minutes. Each day I have a few more, and they're getting stronger in intensity. I don't mind them because they're a reminder that the real thing is close at hand. Besides, they're doing some real good, stretching and thinning the cervix in preparation for the birth. So the more of these I have, the less work my uterus will have to do during real labor (and the faster we'll have to get to the hospital!).

February 10

I'm busy now . . . waiting. There isn't much else to do. Everything is in readiness. I get so tired I'm ready to go back to bed two hours after I get up. I can't stand for any significant length of time or my legs swell painfully. My dignified duck waddle has turned into sort of a lurch—as I get stiff if I stay in one position too long, and then it's an effort to move at all, let alone gracefully. My pelvis feels bruised. I'm not sure if it's because I've been too zealous in doing my exercises, or just another hazard of pregnancy.

I tried riding my bike the other day . . . what a joke! I managed, but I had to go so slow it took twice the effort; I had no momentum. Even worse, my center of balance has shifted (way out front) so that I was incredibly unsteady.

And through it all, even these silly inconveniences are nothing. My spirits are high, I can laugh at myself. I'm ready . . . and waiting.

February 11

What kind of person will you be . . . are you? Will you enjoy the same kinds of things we do? Will you be concerned with people, compassionate?

What kind of mother will I be? Will I be patient, willing to take time to enrich the scope of your life beyond keeping your clothes clean and your body well-fed? Will I also nourish your mind and your heart?

Will I have too many expectations for you, or will I be able to let you grow along your own course, to develop what you already are, or try to mold you into my own hopes? Will I have too many expectations for myself, striving to be Superwoman—the perfect mother, wife, and more?

February 12

Two days from the due date. I don't feel anxious or in a hurry. Since the first month I've made myself believe the baby would arrive two weeks late, and that way avoid the disappointment and anxiety some of my friends have experienced when the magic day arrived and the baby hadn't.

Valentine's Day . . . you're supposed to be here today,
according to the calendar. Everyone calling up . . . "How do
you feel?" "Have you had it yet?" "Why not?" (As if it were
up to me!)

We stayed out way too late last night; one of those
evenings that was planned months ago and by the time it
rolled around no one wanted to do it anymore. I didn't enjoy
it at all.

My short sleep was broken by a series of violent, terrifying
nightmares . . . horrible. I awoke this morning feeling
drained, tired; nothing seems right today.

In my frustration I try to blame George for something—
anything; it doesn't matter what. I just want to get rid of
these awful feelings. But there's nothing to blame him for.
None of it is his fault, anymore than it's anyone else's. All I
do is cry, and probably make him feel awful too . . . which
makes me feel worse.

I'm so tired of looking at myself . . . not my stomach: it
looks beautiful. But my fingers are so puffy I can't wear my
ring. I have a hard time holding a pen. My feet are so swollen
I can't wear shoes. My face is so round it almost disappears
into my neck. I want this to be over. I know I said I didn't
expect it to come today, but I feel pressured. Everyone thinks
it would be wonderful to have a "Valentine Baby." George
supports me though. He knows I can't just sit around and
wait.

I just feel like yelling at the next person who calls and says
"Hi . . ." and then, "well? . . ." I know they're interested
and excited. I just hope I never do that to anybody who's
"waiting."

For the first time I feel like I can't express what I'm feeling.
So many different things push at me from all sides. Pressure,
expectations (mine and others'), fatigue, anticipation, fear of
being a mother, not having any idea how much longer we'll
be waiting . . . everything seems to be coming together all at
once, today, a blanket of emotions smothering me, and all I
want to do is crawl out from under the blanket so I can
breathe, and relax.

Hello . . .

Hi . . . no, not yet. No.

What? Oh I feel fine.

Yes, really. A little tired, but . . .

What?

No, I'm not going crazy,

or feeling anxious.

Uncomfortable? Not too much.

No, I'm really not about to climb the walls.

What?

No, the last month hasn't been bad.

Ride your horse?

No thanks.

A bumpy car ride?

No.

Castor oil? (Yeech!)

No, I don't think so. The baby will come when it's
    ready.

Am I scared?

Of what?

No, why should I be? Why do you think we've
    been going to all these childbirth classes? So
    we'll know what to expect, how to behave.

No. I'm not afraid.

Thanks for calling.

Sure, I promise we'll let you know . . .

Until tonight, the birth has seemed like such a long way away, not quite a reality. Now, suddenly, I feel different, and I don't know why. Everything has suddenly come into focus. I feel ready, and I feel the baby is ready. It's almost intangible. Maybe it will be tonight, maybe not for two weeks. It doesn't matter. I'm ready.

Birth . . .
the first meeting.
The first event
which so perfectly typifies
the experience of
being a parent,
of raising a child,
    of living.
Labor,
    a labor of love,
    yet truly hard work,
somewhat painful
    but less so
      if you can flow with,
      be a part of,
        the process.
One
    can do it alone,
but it usually goes
    much more smoothly
    if both parents
are a team.
And at last,
    the joy,
    the incomparable,
      indescribable joy
of finally experiencing
    the fruit
      of your labor,
        your love . . .

The joy makes it all
worth the work
and the pain . . .

Normally, I am a mediocre houskeeper, at best. My home isn't all that bad, but it would never make Good Housekeeping.

So there must be something to this business of the "nesting instinct." Because suddenly it won't do for my floors to be anything but immaculate, my furniture to be less than glowing, and wonder of wonders, my closets no longer are catch-alls and junk bins.

What's happening to me? Gone are the carefree days of stashing dirty socks in the top desk drawer, sweeping dirt under the handiest piece of furniture, stuffing gum wrappers between the seat cushions and tossing everything I can't find a place for in the nearest closet (and quickly slamming the door so everything else won't come tumbling out)!

As if all this isn't enough: I think it's catching. George actually puts his dirty shorts in the hamper and hangs up his clothes. I no longer see mountains of books and jumbled papers in the den/nursery; everything is neatly filed away.

Amazing . . . I wonder how long it will last?

George has started answering the phone in a new way, to accomodate the incredible number of calls we've been getting. Friends we haven't talked to for six months are calling to check in with us. Everyone seems so interested and excited for us.

The new greeting: "No baby yet!"

3:00 a.m...
Unbelievable! It's happening! I awoke at two this morning feeling somewhat crampy, and somehow I knew that this was it. It's an exhilarating feeling. I started timing contractions and realized what a long way we have to go: 17 minutes apart. We don't even go to the hospital until they're ten minutes apart or less. Oops, another one already? That was ten minutes!

I know I should sleep, but I'm so excited I just had to write something. Besides, I'm hungry. They say you shouldn't eat, but a little plain yogurt can't hurt much. I need the energy.

I can look down at my stomach and see my uterus contracting into a hard ball. A little painful, but a good hurt, like muscles working hard. How can George be so calm and sensible, sleeping away? He knows. I've awakened him for every contraction. It's good he can conserve his energy. Now I'm getting sleepy too. I just had to write though.

Every ten minutes now.
Guess we'd better be going.
Just a couple more to be sure.
OK, let's get going.
Everything all packed.
We're washed, brushed
    and dressed.
Wait . . . no contraction
    this time.
Nope.
Still none.
Well, back to bed.
Snoozing comfortably.
Oops . . . a twinge.
    Too groggy.
Ignore it.
Another . . . and another.
Too strong to ignore now.
But irregular.
Call the doctor.
"Why don't you come on over
    to the hospital?"
Wash your hair?
OK. I'll make the bed.
Call the parents.
I'm so hungry.
And tired.
Can I change my mind?
Can I back out now?
How long will this take?

Two hours of walking the hospital corridor to speed things along, but the contractions keep getting farther apart. I was two centimeters dilated when we came in, and it hasn't changed yet. I concentrate so hard, as if by thinking about it I can make the contractions come harder and faster. Such a feeling of quiet excitement! I'm ready to meet you, baby. Things are moving slowly, but I know the time isn't far away.

They've sent us home. No use in waiting around. It could be hours yet, or even days. The contractions never go away completely. There is always one at least every half hour, usually more often. I'm getting so tired and weak I'm going to have to eat something and just take my chances on getting sick.

This is taking so long, we're both getting a little discouraged. It's almost as though we had our chance at the hospital to have this baby, and we blew it.

One a.m.

My God! So this is it!

There is no comparison between this and what I felt yesterday! These knock me off my feet! I'm calm; I relax for each one. I time them. It takes all my concentration not to be swept under. I drift into a light, tentative sleep. I wake, thrashing, gasping, fighting the pain. I cry to George for help. I haven't wanted to wake him. He's so tired and he'll need every ounce of strength for what lies ahead. But now I need him. Help me. His voice is instantly alert, soothing. "Take a deep breath. Just relax." And I do. It's over. I made it. I'm ready for the next one. It isn't as bad. Finally we dress. There is no real hurry, but this morning I don't make the bed, George doesn't wash his hair.

The sun is rising over the city. We're early enough to miss the traffic. The sky is clear. It's a beautiful day to be born.

They're coming faster and harder now, but I still relax. Some of the same nurses are on duty and they recognize us. I think they also recognize an air of seriousness we didn't possess yesterday. George knows where to wait while I'm being examined. "Three centimetres dilated and fully effaced. We're not going to send you home this time, Mrs. Betts. You're going to have a baby today." I feel a lump in my throat. I can't believe I heard those words! I get my hospital bracelet, sign a stack of forms and settle in to begin my work of relaxing.

Another nurse comes in to examine me. She has been assigned to me now, with the new morning shift. With her is a student nurse, Cindy, who is going to observe me. I resent her presence. I feel like a guinea pig.

The nurse examines me and confirms the facts. Three centimeters. Wait! "That's not the head I feel. That's a soft little butt! Come here, Cindy. Can you feel this?" As Cindy nods, my heart sinks. I try to deny the knowledge of what it probably means. From somewhere I have a vague memory of breech babies and Cesarean Sections. No! It can't be! She's mistaken. She's only a nurse; what does she know? Where is Dr. Bradley? I push the thought away.

They're going to take X-rays to see if the baby has room to come through. A hard table. Harder contractions. Only two to three minutes apart. George waits outside. The X-ray technicians seem to know their job, but they don't seem to know what to do with a laboring mother. My God, will this never end? Hurry, please. Oh wait, just a minute, that was a hard one. The table is standing on end and something warm is running between my legs. "My water has broken. You'd better tell the nurse."

Back in the labor room, George is coaching me, simply saying "relax, take a really deep breath." All our nights of practice were worth every minute, although there is no need for the step-by-step relaxation and fantasy techniques we used in practice. I relax automatically at the sound of his voice. He presses his large, warm hand into the small of my back and the pain almost disappears.

Things begin to happen so quickly. Dr. Bradley arrives, grave and gentle today. The baby is breech. He shows us the X-rays: a perfect human being. We can't tell the sex but we can see the baby is perfectly formed. But I will never dilate enough for it to come out. Dr. Bradley changes his prediction from boy to girl: "Only a girl would be ornery enough to be upside down!" They're going to do a C-Section. I sign more forms. They take the polish off my nails, insert an I.V., shave me and insert a catheter. George is with me and we talk, trying to accept the fact that he can't be with me during the birth. He's ready to cry, and his disappointment makes me want to cry too. But as we talk we gradually accept the fact that it must be this way, and that we'll soon have a baby. They're going to give me a spinal, so I'll be awake during the operation, and George will see the baby when it's about five minutes old.

They take me to the delivery room, which looks like an ordinary operating room to me: cold, green tiles, huge lights, a narrow table to lie on. There isn't even room for my arms. There are five or six nurses bustling around, putting on gowns, getting things ready for the baby. One is pouring water from a bottle into a basin while another counts. What is she counting? Quarts?

I'm beginning to feel like a machine: I.V., catheter, and now a tube in my nose for oxygen and a heart monitor taped to my skin in three places. The nurses ignore me, talking, laughing, busy, except for Cindy, standing quietly, watching. I'm frightened. I'm going to be sick. And still the contractions are coming steadily. No George to soothe me now. Help me!

Doesn't anyone care about me? I can't believe how insensitive they are. I want to cry. I call to Cindy. "Will you put your hand on my back?" She instantly senses my feeling of loneliness and comforts me. She doesn't leave my side again.

Now the doctors are here and things happen so quickly. Dr. Bradley looks so funny in his green cap and gown. The anesthesiologist sits at my head and gently explains the procedure. The pediatrician stands somewhere behind my head. I don't even know what he looks like.

I sit on the side of the table, feet on a high stool, hands on knees, back bent, my head on Cindy's shoulder. A needle is inserted into my spine. Novacaine. Then another. This is the anesthetic. The doctor presses on my back with his finger. It hurts. I lie down. The contractions begin to diminish. My toes feel tingly, and now my feet. I'm draped with sterile sheets. I can't see Dr. Bradley. I want to see what's going on. My legs begin to feel like pins and needles. I can't move them. The table is tilted so my head is lower than my feet. "Tell me when this feels like a pin prick." "I can feel it." "Already?" My head goes lower. "I can feel it now." Lower still. "Yes, I feel that." The anesthetic isn't going high enough. Dr. Bradley injects novacaine deep into my abdomen several times. I feel like a pincushion, but it doesn't hurt. The anesthesiologist suggests they put me to sleep after the baby is born. No! I don't want to go to sleep! Cindy stands next to me, holding my hand.

"What do you see, Cindy?"

"Nothing yet. He's made the first incision."

"Yes, I feel something. It feels like my insides are being

pulled out." But it doesn't hurt. I'm fascinated.

"I see an arm," Cindy tells me, "No a leg. Here it comes. It's a girl! You have a little girl!"

A girl! I don't believe it. She's born! A miracle! I'm crying and so is Cindy.

"Are you in pain?" the doctor asks. "What's wrong?"

"No, she's just happy. I'm crying too," Cindy answers for me. I'm speechless. "Can you hear her?"

"No, I can't."

"Listen, she's crying."

"Yes, now I hear her. Is that really my baby? I want to see her. Where is she?"

The anesthesiologist inserts something into the I.V. "Is that going to put me to sleep? I don't want to go to sleep. Not till I see her." I don't go to sleep. They show her to me, and I'm crying again. A real live person, who just came from inside me.

I'm getting tired now, but I don't go to sleep. I'm in the recovery room. George is with me. "I've seen her, and she's beautiful!" I don't believe him. All newborn babies seem beautiful, but they aren't really. How could she be different?

They're yelling at me. "Take a deep breath, Mrs. Betts. Push my fist out with your chest. A deep breath!" I don't want to. I'm tired and it's too much trouble. But they keep yelling at me. I try. It takes all my strength to breathe. I want to go to sleep. I'll breathe later, when I feel better. An oxygen mask. It almost hurts to breathe. I keep trying, but I don't want to. No, I can't wiggle my toes. Don't be silly. They're dead. I can't feel them, but I know they're there. I come out of my stupor to hear George saying how beautiful she is. I see three other mothers, and they're all holding their babies. I resent them. Why can't I have my baby?

They wheel me to my room, and everyone is standing in the hall: my mom and dad, George's mom, Viddie. I say something to them, but I don't remember what. Now they are asking me to climb into a bed. They must be crazy! My stomach feels like it's coming open. I sleep now, but they are still trying to coax a deep breath from me. George is with me and he asks if I want to see the baby. No, later, when I wake up. But here she comes. He had asked the nurses to bring her, so the three of us could share our first meeting. He was so right.

Hello, Kristina. Oh, she really is beautiful! Not ordinary baby-beautiful, but really lovely. She has lots of dark hair, like George, a creamy complexion and rosy cheeks. She's so alert. A nurse comes in and I ask if I can nurse her. She helps me. Here is my daughter at my breast, and suddenly all the love and excitement that's been building for the last nine months comes in a flood of joy. Kristina, my angel, I love you. You are perfect, you are beyond anything I'd ever dreamed of. I never knew I could love you so much in an instant. I can't describe my joy, my sense of total fulfillment. Our first meeting, just the three of us.

George is bursting with happiness. We had both wanted a little daughter so much we had hardly dared to hope. Oh George, thank you for the baby.

February 25

The first thing this morning they brought Kristi's picture to me, taken the day she was born. I look at it and burst into tears. Oh, thank you God. Oh, she's so beautiful, so perfect. She's here. Is she really real? How can I be so lucky? Thank you, thank you. I love her so much I can only cry in joy.

They bring her to me, and the tears flow again as I hold her to me. She's so beautiful I can't look at her, or I cry even harder. My little Kristi, I love you so much.

All day, just thinking about her makes me start to cry again, in happiness.

George is so wonderful and so happy. He brought me a bottle of perfume, a surprise he's had planned for months. I cry again. I'm so lucky to have him.

I watch him hold Kristi, his face a picture of adoration. I've never seen this in him before. I love him all the more, and I cry again. So already little Kristi is teaching us about love!

The nurses here are so kind, so helpful. This is the second day that one of them has spent nearly all morning teaching Kristi and me how to nurse (it's something we both have to learn). Without their help I would have given up long ago. But what a beautiful feeling to know that my body can still sustain Kristi completely. She has not had any nourishment except what comes from my body; no supplement of any kind. And what a peaceful feeling I have when I look down and see this tiny bundle of love sucking contentedly. My heart could burst.

February 28

I'm so lonely for George tonight. I go home tomorrow, but I can't stand this loneliness. The blues have struck, I guess. The nurse found me crying in bed and I asked if she would bring Kristi to me. Kristi and I cuddled most of the night, and her tiny presence was an incredible comfort . . .

George was so excited today as he helped Kristi and me dress
for our trip home. I knew it must be something special.
George tenderly ushered me into the house, Kristi in his
arms, and he was bursting with pride at what he had done:
the house was immaculate, there were bouquets of carnation
in every room (arranged by him). By our bed were *three*
yellow roses and a poem. But I thought he would burst as he
brought me his masterpiece: a beautiful white-on-white cake
(my favorite) bearing the words "Welcome Home, Donni and
Kristi." I have never felt so welcome in my own home.

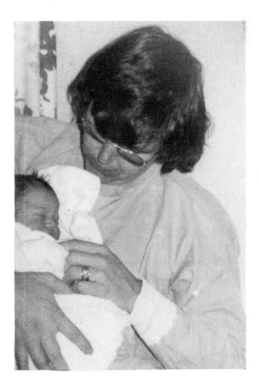

There is no way anyone could ever have prepared me for the tremendous amount of time, energy and emotion necessary to care for a small baby; no way.

Kristi, you've been awake for five hours this evening, and during that time I have nursed you, changed you, played with and amused you, rocked you, talked and sung to you, and changed you again. It's been tiring. I have wanted to do other things.

And yet, it's been rewarding. Even in this one evening I've watched you learn to focus on faces and toys, and I've heard your first coos and babbles; seemingly small things to an outsider, but for us they are the first of uncountable achievements.

No wonder you are too exhausted to sleep. No wonder I feel as though I've been in a five-hour wrestling match. And yet I do all of this gladly, because I realize how lucky I am to witness the blossoming of a new life, and because I love you so.

So many people have said what a shame it is that George and I worked so hard in preparation for natural childbirth, only to have wasted our time. I don't feel that way at all.

I am so happy to have had the chance to prepare and to learn so much about my body and the birth process. Also, I was in labor for 30 hours, and our nights of relaxation practice were definitely not in vain. Without such training I would have been fighting my body, rather than working with it, and I would have endured a great deal of pain.

Even more important, because George and I knew how to behave, we were calm and rational and able to deal with our feelings when confronted with the prospect of a C-Section. Had I been tense or anxious, the doctor told me he would have had to put me to sleep and I would never have experienced the climactic moment of Kristi's birth.

Another reason I'm grateful for our training: I was so calm and so successful at relaxing, and I had done it long enough that I know, beyond any doubt, that no matter how much stronger the contractions became, I could have given birth without medication. That was very important to me. I had to know, and now I do: I could have made it . . .

March 24

Here I go, trying to be Super-wife and Super-mom. I'm not doing too badly with the mothering but I feel like I'm falling down on the wife job. I catch myself trying to do everything and feeling guilty when I don't.

I tried to arrange it so George and I could go out alone, something we haven't done since Kristi was born. But I made it seem like such a big deal that George lost his patience. My feelings are mixed: on one side, I resent him losing his temper, not realizing how hard it is for me, and most of all taking advantage of the freedom I don't feel I have: just being able to get up and walk out the door.

On the other hand, he's been so patient and helpful, how much can I ask of him?

I think I've made the whole adjustment seem easier than it's really been. Somehow I haven't communicated to George what a mental upheaval it's been. I find I can no longer order my thoughts, think straight, see what needs to be done around the house, or even carry on an intelligent conversation. Because EVERYTHING is different. Every facet of my life in relation to the world has suddenly changed: my body, my values, my roles, my relationships with people, my time schedule, my activities; there is nothing that hasn't changed.

And because everything I do has to be approached from a

new angle, everything becomes a big deal and I have trouble planning more than an hour ahead of time.

I think George expects our lifestyle to change very little, though. He still seems to want to go out every night, always be doing something. I feel like we've got to slow down some.

And then today I realized how hard all of this must be on him too. I feel it's up to me to make sure he doesn't feel neglected. I feel guilty and overwhelmed all at once. So much responsibility. I need help.

March 31

When Kristi is nursing I look at her and feel a sudden rush of peace, of contentment, pure love. It's a pleasure I've never known before, a feeling of completeness. I hope that my feelings are somehow transmitted to Kristi through my touch, the emotion of my voice, my milk, any way, just so she may experience the feelings I have. I am sure that because of this, she will grow into a stronger, more secure and giving person and I am thankful I can be a part of it.

Being a mother brings out all the insecurities I feel about myself. I want so much to do my best at mothering. I sometimes wonder if I am and I sometimes know I'm not.

I have a philosphy about parents and children which I think is going to help me to accept Kristi's growing up in a graceful way. We are most dependent on our parents at birth. At that moment we begin a continual process of gaining independence and in that way growing away from our parents. It's natural and necessary although sometimes pain-ful. I can see signs of it in Kristi, already. But I also see that as she grows and gains independence, my respect and admira-tion for her as her own person grow too, and I feel closer to her, love her a little more every day.

I never realized until now how selfish I am: I have always jealously guarded my private time, the kind of time I don't seem to have these days.

It's the little things I miss, like taking a bath or reading an article or writing in my book, with no interruptions except the ones I choose to heed. Again I emphasize that although I was aware of the possibility of this kind of lifestyle before Kristi arrived, I was not prepared for what it would mean to me. I always blithely assured myself that although my friends chose to arrange their lives that way, I would do better! Ha!

But it's a challenge, and one I am rising to. My day sometimes seems like a juggling act, but I am learning to find ways for Kristi to amuse herself so that I can have longer stretches of uninterrupted time to do the things I need to do. The only conflict is that she is usually so cute when she amuses herself, cooing and smiling, that I'm tempted to forget the other things and play with her. Then I end up in frustration.

I'm also learning to be more relaxed in my approach to life: I don't always fall apart when I don't get everything done. So I'm also learning to take time to relax, to really enjoy Kristi's babyhood, rather than trying to hurry her through a feeding or rush her into sleep. This little person is teaching me so many important things about life, and about myself.

April 11

I know the time will come when I look at you and realize you're no longer a baby. I know it because I see signs of change in you every day. So I treasure your babyhood all the more. You are innocence, freshness, simplicity amid the complexities of life. You bring me back from artificiality and superficiality to the purity of your uncomplicated world.

You are springtime.

April 29

In glancing through some of the things I've written since the beginning of the pregnancy, I find that I have experienced many of the things that I so feared, and yet now that the whole experience of being a parent is a reality, I find that there is not all that much to fear. It's true, there have been times when I've felt trapped, cut off from the world, or frustrated when I find myself faced with so little time and so many things I want to do. And yet somehow I make it through each day in fine shape. In fact, I find that that is exactly how I must live right now—one day at a time. And I treasure each day all the more . . . each one is special. The main reason is because I see so many changes in you each day. I've always heard people say that a baby changes every day, but now I believe it.

And the feelings of closeness I shared with you while I was pregnant are still there, only magnified. For now when I hold you and feel your warmth and your trust, you smile back at me and I feel as though I could melt.

Yes, it's awesome to feel that I am still your total world, but at the same time, knowing that you trust me completely to make your day and your world right for you has given a purpose, a special meaning to each day.

May 1

You're nearly ten weeks old Kristina, and I still feel as though you were born only yesterday. The memory of the time just before and during your birth is still vivid. In spite of the physical pain and the disappointment of not being able to bring you into the world "naturally," your birth is still one of the most profound, moving moments of my life. I wish I could experience it again, for now that I know you and love you as a person, a reality, and not just a dream, it seems I could feel the glory of that moment even more totally.

And yet, maybe it's one of those rare, fleeting moments in life that can be appreciated fully only in retrospect . . .

September 3

The notion of home birth seems to be getting more popular all the time. People are more willing to give up some of the miracles of science to recapture the miracle of a "natural" birth in the comfortable, familiar surroundings of their own home.

Although I don't love hospitals, I have never felt the dislike for them that some people have expressed, and I had no objection to having my baby in one. In fact it never really occurred to me to do otherwise. I guess I wasn't willing to make any compromises in relation to the safety of my baby. And in spite of a few lonely moments in the delivery room, I'm so thankful for that decision. If I had chosen to have my baby at home, the chances are there would be no Kristi . . .

A good lesson, but such a painful one . . . for all of us. How often do we, as parents, strive to do the best, and maybe fall short by doing *too* much, *too* well?

Tonight George had to work late, and I had the rare luxury of joining him for dinner—without Kristi. My parents kept her. I felt giddy while getting ready to go; it was a date, an adventure. All through dinner I was keenly aware of the enjoyment I felt at being apart from Kristi. I love my private time and I have so little of it these days. After dinner George went back to work, and rather than hurrying home to Kristi as I had planned, I called Dad to say I wanted to do some shopping. He told me Kristi was really crying so I offered to come home. But he insisted I go ahead with my plans.

Every store was like a new discovery. I was elated. I bought nearly everything I saw that I wanted, on impulse; something I rarely do. I bought presents for everyone: George, Mom, Dad, Kristi, myself. It seemed like Christmas.

And as I wandered the aisles I was realizing how good it felt to be away from Kristi, to miss her a little, to be able to reflect on my role as a mother, from a distance. Circumstances had not permitted me to do this lately, and I vowed to get away more.

After two and a half hours of shopping I returned home, eager to share my treasures. George was home already. Everyone was glad to see my excitement, but there was tension in the air. Finally it came: Kristi had *screamed* for two and a half hours, probably with grief at the disappearance of me, her mother, the center of her life. I had been gone five hours, probably the longest we've been separated, ever. Five hours. And she fell apart. With her loving, patient grandparents. She stopped screaming when her daddy came home.

I saw my baby, six months old, her eyes red and swollen from crying, her breath coming in shudders from so much sobbing, and suddenly all my motherly confidence crumbled: What had I done wrong? I knew the problem did not lie in leaving her, but in not leaving her more often, and longer.

What is wrong with me, I cried inwardly, that has made me become so wrapped up in this little person. I had made her the center of my world, too. And now, doubting my own actions, my world was crumbling. I saw examples everywhere of how I had devoted myself to her, and I felt embarrassed: spending so much time with her, taking her everywhere with me, buying her so many pretty things, nursing her so devotedly, even writing this book. And for a few moments it all seemed wrong. This morning I had been telling myself what a good mother I am, and suddenly I felt like a horrible, smothering mother. Everything which had been so right was suddenly wrong.

But after thinking it over for a couple of hours I realized that's not true either. Kristi is a dream come true; she's everything I ever hoped for and even more. She's like a favorite painting that suddenly becomes life-like: there is so much more to be delighted with in the three-dimensional; so many facets to uncover and explore.

And in my joy at having my dream come true I have been striving to do and be the best: yes, Supermom! In a way I have been successful: Kristi is happy, healthy and secure . . . when she's with *me*. But I haven't given her the chance to feel that way with others often enough. And by the same token I feel those things with her; but my world is limited too. I haven't been kind enough to me, taken time for myself.

So I see that I haven't really failed . . . I just got carried away. And I realized these things on my own, while I was shopping. But the realization was made more dramatic when I came home to that tearful scene.

So now the problem is: how to undo some of the dependency, or rather interdependency, that we have created. One of the main factors is the nursing. A month ago it was an important, even necessary thing to me emotionally, and I felt to Kristi, both emotionally and physically.

But in the last few days I've begun to feel that the nursing is beginning to outlive its purpose: Kristi is growing older, becoming more interested in other food and other people, and I am beginning to feel restless, in need of other involvement.

At the same time, nursing has been such a valuable, gratifying part of my life for six and a half months. It has provided closeness, warmth and security for me as well as Kristi. And I have the knowledge that I have been giving Kristi the best possible nutrition, protecting her body from disease and allergies, and just providing her with the best start in life. At the same time, I have been able to extend some of the peaceful feelings of my pregnancy, by preserving the physical bond we shared, and knowing I am using my body's full potential for the purpose for which it was designed.

So nursing has been a powerful and total experience, physically and emotionally for both Kristi and me. I know this tender, joyful, fulfilling chapter of my life is coming to a close. And although it's good and right for it to be this way, I feel some sadness too. There is no way I can recapture the experience. It means Kristi is growing out of her babyhood. It's right and natural, and I so eagerly await the next stage, and yet I love her this way too. This must be the dilemma of parenthood: The ambiguity which brings such joy and sadness at the same time; the lifelong journey of watching someone we love, created from our love, move from one poignant stage of her life to the next . . . loving her and yet knowing we must let her be . . .

I have never been the kind of person who adores everyone else's kids. Even when I was pregnant I wasn't eager to hold other babies. I think I was afraid they might cry, and that would mean they disliked me. But somehow I know that I would feel different about my own, and I do: I'm confident, not afraid of her. And although I *do* adore her, I still don't adore everyone else's, but I am more open to them. There is just a special bond that exists, and I suspect my feelings are fairly common.

I kiss Kristi every night before I go to bed, as though my kiss is protection that will keep her safe through the night.

The other day I expressed the feeling that everything about Kristi has been perfect from the moment of her conception, except her birth. I hadn't quite accepted the Cesarean, although I knew that somehow it must fit into the total experience too.

I feel it is resolved now, at last. I am at peace with this too. I realize that I was meant to have Kristi this way. True, I have felt sadness, even felt I was cheated. I was *never* to experience the glory of giving birth.

In the past when people knew of my C-Section they would sympathize, "Oh, what a shame. You must have been terribly disappointed." And I would agree. But I no longer feel that way. I realize that this too, is a gift I must share. Through my education and past experience I have gained the skills to share feelings and to bring understanding. I'm not quite sure how yet, but I intend to use these skills to help other families who are faced with a difficult birth to come to terms with their situation, to see it in a positive light, and to find meaning and beauty in their own unique, if painful, experience.

And now that Kristi is six months old, how do I feel about being a mother? I have expressed a great deal of anticipation, some fears and doubts, and so much hope for joy and fulfillment.

For the most part my fears were unfounded. Kristi is an almost constant source of joy. I seldom feel limited, as I was so afraid I would. True, I have little time for myself, but it's a situation I have created, partly because I want to share my time with my family, and mostly because I am poorly organized.

If I was concerned that Kristi would come between the relationship George and I value so much, I need not have worried so. She has added a new dimension to our life, given it a freshness; another aspect for us to share. She has made us more complete. But we are going to have to work harder at giving more attention to each other and not so much to Kristi. She is so exciting to watch, always on the verge of some new skill or discovery. Whoever thought we could be so fascinated with watching someone discover their hands, and then learning to use them for pat-a-cake? Not me!

Somehow I feel at a loss for words to describe the complete and total joy I feel in the gift that is Kristi. I think it is such a personal, unique experience that it can't be described, only experienced uniquely by each person, each family. It is the privilege of the shared journey of life.

November 3

I know I'll remember this night years from now. There is nothing spectacular about tonight. We have celebrated no birthdays; it isn't a holiday. And yet it is special for me, in a quiet, private way.

Long after you had gone to sleep, I crept into your room to put away some of your little things. As I entered I felt a peacefulness in your room. It not only smells as fresh and clean as it looks; there is a purity, a simplicity in the air. You looked so innocent lying in your crib. Yet around your eyes I sense a hint of the woman inside you, waiting to emerge as your future unfolds. It's something I never see when you are awake and busy exploring your world, but only when your eyes are closed and you are quiet. And then I wonder what kind of life you will have, what you will be like. And I feel that years from now, when you are grown, I will sometime gaze down on you as you sleep, and fondly think of tonight.

BIOGRAPHY FOR A SHARED JOURNEY

Since the birth of her child Donni Betts has become actively involved in the study of family-centered Cesarean Birth. She is a member of the Childbirth Preparation Association of Colorado. She is also a member of the Cesarean Birth Support Group, an organization providing support and education for families expecting or experiencing Cesarean Birth, to promote a more positive, family-centered experience.

She teaches a class entitled "Mothers Are People Too," for new mothers who wish to make the most of their roles as wife and mother and still retain a sense of self.

In addition, she is involved in individual and group counseling in the field of personal growth and self-enhancement. With her husband, George, she created "Growing Together: A Workshop for Couples." They co-authored the book GROWING TOGETHER. At this time Donni is completing an M.A. in Psychology, Counseling and Guidance.

If you are interested in sharing your own ideas and experiences, send your letters to Donni Betts, c/o Celestial Arts, 231 Adrian Road, Millbrae, Ca. 94030.